JUST IN: WORD OF
NAVIGATIONAL
CHALLENGES

by Ed Roberson

When Thy King Is a Boy (1970)
Etai-Eken (1975)
Lucid Interval as Integral Music (1985)
Voices Cast Out to Talk Us In (1995)
Just In: Word of Navigational Challenges (1998)

JUST IN:
WORD OF
NAVIGATIONAL
CHALLENGES

NEW AND SELECTED WORK

To Shannon
Best Wishes
09/21/00

ED ROBERSON

Ed Roberson

Talisman House, Publishers
Jersey City, New Jersey

Published in the United States of America by
Talisman House, Publishers
P.O. Box 3157
Jersey City, New Jersey 07303-3157

Manufactured in the United Sates of America
Printed on acid-free paper

The sections from *Lucid Interval as Integral Music* and "Aerialist Narratives"
are reprinted by permission of the University of Iowa Press.

Library of Congress Cataloging-in-Publication Data

Roberson, Ed.
    Just in : word of navigational challenges : new and selected work
/ Ed Roberson.
       p.   cm.
    ISBN 1-883689-80-5 (cloth : alk. paper). — ISBN 1-883689-79-1
(paper : alk. paper)
    I. Title. II. Title: Word of navigational challenges.
PS3568.O235J8 1998
811'.54—dc21
                                          98-45418
                                           CIP

CONTENTS

v

vii

JUST IN: WORD OF NAVIGATIONAL CHALLENGES

from WHEN THY KING IS A BOY (1970)

be careful

i must be careful about such things as these.
the thin-grained oak.   the quiet grizzlies scared
into the hills by the constant tracks squeezing
in behind them closer in the snow.   the snared
rigidity of the winter lake.   deer after deer
crossing on the spines of fish who look up and stare
with their eyes pressed to the ice.   in a sleep.   hearing
the thin taps leading away to collapse like the bear
in the high quiet.   i must be careful not to shake
anything in too wild an elation.   not to jar
the fragile mountains against the paper far-
ness.   nor avalanche the fog or the eagle from the air.
of the gentle wilderness i must set the precarious
words.   like rocks.   without one snowcapped mistake.

there is against explicit stating what

there is against explicit stating what things are
the family of instants born to a happening,
the multiple thunder of the number of their hearts:
the fly buzzing against the window and the plane
that for the lack of just that character
somewhere is going down.   there is a child somewhere
who screams in an amusement park   whose hands,
begging the heavens for this balloon,   have just dispatched
the dark zepplins against the english night.
and in the countryside the circumstance
adds a spoon of dull explosion to the tea
and at the same time in france there falls a rain
adding to what already is without any relation
except perhaps the stupid sea
the continents move in . . .

i am afraid that some hand not my own
may rise and answer present to my name,
that some me might debate me on this button
i have been careless these years pinning on,
leaving an unowned grasp its emptiness.
i am afraid my fine foot may not answer
'slender' 'warm' slow arched one of these mornings
as it should, because it had awakened
here too soon.   taking one early step
into tomorrow tomorrow i am not in.

news

1

the news is covered

today brought to you
by the same coverage

as smothered yesterday

There is this to say
there is no stillness
if there is a voice

announcing this
is stillness
It is broken i have broken

this piece just to still
closer to stillness
An Absence

2

in its   role as an important part
in the play of time information has
the latest word has been pronounced dead.

causes are that cause as what was felt
to first have moved the feeler to the subject
he is now is not to be performed

objection which the bug movements of interest
weave a coverage and lay opinions
towards a blossoming that bursts with time

and time's diversity of rots

[3]

3

it can never be said
a mob was made by this
voice with its intension
in delivery
so it can never be said
we return you now
to the news with any truth

4

the news is brief
as air   as light
as paper is how it arrives
tho it is all the headstone

this population of voice
and ancient filigreed face
of type concerns
you   with you

5

top official for the purposes
of top   security has released
lies   defining a position
the whirl of balances will even
not let stand

              on his side
the this side   up points on
to the horizon as the subject
turns and backs out of sight

news continued   release

rescue workers fought today
and yesterday another day today
in efforts to avert the same
tomorrow. one eye witness on the scene
reported and the wide effects
opened a decade in the wrecks
of sequences supposed under control.
official estimates of toll
have been suppressed for purposes of piece
by piece attention to belief.
authorization to the area
is given as is birth to myriads.

report

the subject was reported seen
facing a window at what seemed
to be a late reflection.

proprietors deny the window
or that anything at all
is in it anyhow.

a witness has been found who cost
his findings which were lost
among his life

but whose holdings are not official.
victims are advised
to pass or be satisfied.

it

it has scratched shadows
angels that meant its passing   on my gate
it has bent down my stalk of sun
until the bloom breaks off behind the hill
it has stuck wads of breath into
a toy man sickness had played with
one game after another
and it has looked in one man's eye
and was not seen to walk away

what has gone on with it behind the doors
that, closed off, define me in this building
i am jealous of
and print upon the door
                              a hall is spent
taking what we are called between us yet

its boot crossing the same field
              has brought to mud
the hard earth finally
a day nothing can get through but that it enters

the sole irrhythm II.

i.

owners of what they own
under the unescapable
deed of singular skin
ask their two genetic salesmen who
have watched the plot that they by two had let
break and escape
what country they are in.

the sea has stolen grain by grain
the letters of the sand
the breakers can be heard deciding
formally the order of the vowels.
and simply as the hours play into night,
through the walls
the son has robbed his father's bed
eaten by ear the plundered and become like him.
the striking amulets on his belly.

a name unweaves on reaching the intestines.
the title of the kingdom still unknown.
for all his violence,
the headdress unidentified . . .

ii.

straightened from the sleep the form of egg
the chin is lifted from the clavicle
into the upright of its pride the pillow
of the chest is stuffed with musculature
and air has laid its head on it.
now the years have put them to   expect
the orbs to be their potent, the sceptre
its damascus of perfection, these
together a right

iii.

the legs are such precarious things
exposed foundations ivied down with hair
the casings rock has evolutions over
deserted and left bare.
time will termite into them
and chance flood them under accident.

on champions the formal masonry
is prone to come unmarried at the seams
the loose torso upon the seasonless bough
heavily intestined with dark worms.

i am a lot concerned about my body.
all its rooms.   and all the rhythms tapped
out on its walls that answer back
in moving
the trapped in occupant toward death.
the sole irrhythm in the brain
never answering why.

[9]

the sole irrhythm III., iii.

iii.

. . . there is a corner just ahead whose turning
is so badly understood that being
upset is included in the tickets.
the beauties of the track are well known words,
the lines which evenings run gold to the sun.
but just inside the glare — the cornering:
the architecture of its wreckages
a depot out of nowhere with its hook
to make the harshest of transactions with the parcels
down from the naive hills.
the coaches come and on them
all the peopling of the one-eyed race,
so many beardless pelts compartmented
to make the business of the merchant flies
so easy in the last bazaar of spoilage in the sun

iv.

one corner short of the horizon

18,000 feet

how these loose rocks got piled up here like this
where everything below builds up so steadily —
     a swoop a day long countries wide increases
     from deeper green into a paler leaning
     ice   then to this small pile and finally
     to room for each of us one at a time
     careful   of the cracking of the flag.
how piece by piece   stepped beyond   the element
of left and right   taken away, the sense of here
is made   all there is
under the feet,   all to come   down
how much a prison freedom is
to what is   i
     learned

dreaming has made more strict the terms of dreaming

dreaming has made more strict the terms
of dreaming.   the coinage of confusion
in towers i regret is spread
on an expensive bed.   the difference
becomes a harder thing to purchase
                  at the market evening
some forms are shown to be those of the moon
now whore to habits that were
                  once free with the darkness.
a used to be light   cutting off
tying down or not allowing in
has had a dream's hangers ripped away
and by the terrible tradition that is
creates the term of eunuch for what is to be.
                  o buyer
what is on the mind is not easy
to come right out and tell you   certain things
and dreams not finished to the point
of final polished starting up   and screaming
            sat up in bed all at once
dull   ended in no dream at all.
          except the one
that it was   on there hard   whatever it was
to tell you   sits you
            up too
            dulls you
            ends you know
because there are no certain things.
because to dream is not to dream
            if waking up is never finished
            the terms never fulfilled

Four Lines of A Black Love Letter Between Teachers

bored. confused actually. have started several letters.
usually about   4 in the morning wch is to say something
about my tenancy in the house of sleep/black.
evicted. universal. wch is to say 'There's a certain
                              amount of traveling
wch is to say   in a dream deferred.'
i taught Langston Hughes today.   Same In Blues.
and my soul/*stoppt before the mirror at my body sleeping in the
white-*
     ness of the moon . . .

brought it back. saved   newspaper then lost it
waking up. about the confrontation hate
the loss of meaning in that word) between the black
students and the president   of the campus the folks made him
look like a fool. he is   retreating into his power bag
more jab about in loco parentis do you dig it tsk tsk

there is something about music in this letter. mmm how you do me
this heh way. but the lecture was music   you know
i got so many bags i can only read they faces
from inside. run out   of labels even fore
i run me out of words   wch is to say
/descriptions   there's that refrain again
wch of the wch ways to gone   and say . . . /black

a classical problem lawd
i/s here by mysef
got no company. what I got
/i
already got. what i know
i know
why i bother with puttin it down. nuthin
nobody else know   wch is to say.
all you all/you people why you want it down   this way
i was about to attend a sinkin. when yall showed up with the hole
. . . mmmiss you baby

[13]

you ask was it all right. i said yes wch is to say.
i didn't say (to you no. no is not
a pill. quinine nor enovid. yes is. for me.
tastes weird as anything else
about us put a hair
on my hope maybe my chest. but thas oright.

been loving other men's sons lately:
buying toys for students' sons on my way to dinner
don't take much to get an A from me.
hey hey you there baby at the end of this line
let me be yo sidetrack till yo mainline come
i can do more switchin than yo mainline
done now   students about presumption. 'A certain
                                        amount of nothing
1   Ibid.,   in a dream deferred.'
2   vid., next refrain.
3   ad int./cf., today is a   .sine loco(:op.cit.,
4   i.e., i am   watering an irish rose.   ooop pop a dop bop

i've lost the letter of this act.
with a pun as multiple as that.
"theys liable to be confusion."
to write   a love letter for someone else
to you the one i love
is a love   in a where someworld sometime else
done now
so signed if this is the night, who else but but
is it   black
but look/here look here one more
thing. every new love adds   to the meaning of love any lingering
love old love
has to catch up even to linger. so you're going to have
his black baby

[14]

war song sing

i do not sit in your mouth
    to take your beauty.
do not let your tongue poison me.
i will not leave your mouth
    dry of words.
do not shut your sharp teeth on my pen.
i will not stench your mouth
    with my starvation.
do not drink the last of my blood.
do not sew the pussy of your mouth
    closed with lies
here i learn the dowry of my own words.

song

i know about the woods you know.
you know i knew the bark who was the sun.
i thought was me.
the rough around the bodies of the oars.
i know how to say the things you know.
you know i never had a whole lot to say.
what i won't leave my sons about carving
was never in the mind of wood.

you know i know how you sleep you know.
i know how to
i know you got to have 1
i know how my 2 keep me awake.
never one when one numbers the shore of order.
i know what   about myself   you know.
and what my eyes don't look like in the water
never hunted the night.

i know simply   you know
enough to be caught skipping backwards
the smooth stone in a mountain   over no river
without surprise or move   from state to state.
i know the wood simply
the tree is   a wreck   of the ash of the watchfire
what i know that is not a stranger
was never in the mind of order.   of the woods.

the next song

i paid my becoming well not to become.
and now gain even to gain my life
's a hole in the hungry pocket of my skin.
and all points between these two are points
opened in that skin and closed there one way:
and any shot   either life or last of thieves
's the opposite of bleeding . and not healed
and not you i am the sieve and not your friend.

On The Calligraphy of Black Chant

i paid my becoming well not to become
i paid
i paid my becoming
      my becoming
               well
      my becoming well
i paid my becoming well not to
i paid my becoming well not to become.
and now gain even to gain my life
and now
and now gain
        gain even to gain
           even to gain my life
and now gain
's a hole
  a hole in the hungry pocket
         the hungry
              gain
's a hole in the hungry pocket of my skin.

and all points between these two are points
and all points
and all points between these two
and all points between these two are points
points opened
opened in that skin
opened in that skin and closed there
opened in that skin and closed there
                      one way!
opened in that skin and closed there one way.
's the opposite of bleeding   one way:
and any shot   either life or last of thieves
's the opposite of bleeding

is the opposite of bleeding and not healed
                  and not healed

and not you
            i am the sieve
                        and not healed
and not you i am the sieve
                        and not your friend.
            i am the sieve
                        and not healed
and not you i am the sieve and not your friend.
            i am the sieve and not your friend.
            i am the sieve
            i am the sieve

When Thy King Is A Boy

Woe to thee, O land, when thy king is a boy,
And thy princes feast in the morning.
                                    Eccles. 10:16

I.

i frog prince have sunk more into the change
than the simple dip of love or coin
those ungreen clods mudfill the wish vein with.
green i leaned in like these need never try.
the small kiss that a frog has   taken in
the moon's face on the water   breaking up
and swallowing the coin i am thrown in.
no wish not even practice love   granted
me.   only the well's slug of my lasting
green and lack returned me.   me taken
in that hand those having are not dealt
by that sharp   intact they needn't meet
that term they filthily them   needn't try striking.

i frog prince in my poorness put to change
more than a wealthless organ and a face.
a whole estate of what wishes could be
wished from all i could be as a frog.
left this miscoined patience   i am
after all a prince   eventually.
she came

II.

(amor vincet omnes, sleeping beauty!

there never comes the so desired beginning
that somewhere does not trip in its procession
somewhere that won't include mis-invitations
to a few slow legged drawbacks who string
the liberation to continuum.
there never sounds a bell that does not bring
the old hour with it or the minute thing
of its old rule that swings it soon back dumb.
the sure event to make things different
is come and so much better than believed
has done itself.   but one love in its bed
does not law love the prick machine of these
bubbles of to be undone worlds nor wed
that stiff win to the after it has spent.

III

what i do love will prove just enough
til more than what enough was when we tried
our cause is committed by its done.
i will set worlds right in your bed tonight
i have your look and see that says that done
is precedent   that do the only source.
i have your look and see   and see that read that read
and read   leaks how the lien on love is done.
but when i end over into sleep
what plaintiff of a lover underneath
our world has not had his and sues toward ours.
what full one doesn't ends us shy because
no one who knew knows why when it has done
doing what does   it was not what to do

IV

(l'etat c'est moi)

1

The king has fallen to the raw belief
in women for his ills.   and time is ill
          to him. so naked
on the table lies the state
in its affairs   and balanced tendencies
          it takes to grip a woman
while the hemorrhoid hunter has his finger
          chambered in the puzzle

of the lay anatomy.   it is
believed the two are covered under one
          embracing policy
after which unarmed arrangement naked
          on the table rests
in its flagging insurances the state
          of impotence and dragging
beauty tripping on its (40's) was.

twentyone: they were once. they two bared
for each others' stethoscopic nip
          of breast — but that is over.
it has fallen to the raw belief
that rung, its grabbing up calls living
          to the line   out of
the smart or moldy snatch of talk.
and it has come   to this.

2

two bitches.

3

under the subtle pimp of silken
organization   girlishly fell the state
                in patients' dream
of safety into danger in the sheets
                of taken care of
businesses only the proper undoing
gets done and retaped in the red knot of want not
                taken care of

under the supple silk of pimping
organizing its mannishness feels the state
                under mons veneris
of tape its real anatomy   and hates
                the smooth new bed it has
erected to its swollen office

4

stabs itself on this disorder
                palms off
the joseph's blood for wedding stains

convenes its ancestral physicians
                with a pride
of flags all roaring maned

lies down and waits the upshot
                of the fall
from the mount.already named
                the (grievish) father.

5

The king before the king all their long night
        had not become the father
of the future he had thought.   the son
       remained unknown.
and by the heavy walk of the clouds
of his own doubt
           it could not be forecast
    if the sun so late carried
    so high might not be blackened hell.

and we have entertained his nakedness
with just that other bitch of his own
      nakedness.
probing its own probe all their long night.

6

and it has come to this
        simply the king
        has put his night in.
        applied to a wound
        inside himself.

        that he knows
        is the cunning window the
          mystery
        all he is come through.

7

The only
social object is
"a man, carved
out of himself"

and under that
stone
the state miscarries.

8

"And it shall be assigned unto.
You shall find   to come   conspicuous
enough, lying in the moment
king . . ."

9

Now there came to the king the questioner
and asked if it were day or were it night.
the king looked in the mirror at the son
and said he was himself. as for his own
he could not say who owned the crown or where
inside the nigger mirror his line hid.
the questioner walked in him to his bath
and floated in his lap. and its one eye
dry of the glances it had hit him with
turned to the queen as he thought she came in.

he hung his towel and ended toward the day
                of business with the state.

jacket

jacket

many of these poems attempt to make
happen to words   that which happens
to lines

                in an optical illusion
many of these lines have.   that.

kind of architecture of
things which live in the sea
they are built
,without a base
beginning above
the ordinary ground of the mind
and ending   there in
illusion

yet they are not
illusions they are
real because the poetic of all (our languages
has the more potential for concretion
it can be said that

"Many of these poems attempt to make
happen to words that which happens
to lines in an optical illusion.
Many of these poems have that.
kind of architecture of
things which live in the sea
They are built without a base.
beginning above

the ordinary   ground of the mind
and ending   there in

[27]

illusion. Yet   they are not illusions. They are
real because   the potential of all our languages
has the more potential for concretion.
It can be said that either these poems
recognize   their suspension so clearly
concretize   their suspension so graphically
OR from   their suspension
recognize   the ground   so clearly
that the glaregularity / clarity of that vision
has created
such   a solid about itself that that.
chaos   is the real ground" — Mr. Roberson
writes — Ed Roberson is not a real poet.

and further: Many of these poems attempt to make happen to words
that which happens to lines in an optical illusion. Many of these
poems have that kind of architecture of things which live in the sea.
They are built without a base, beginning above the ordinary ground of
the mind and ending there in illusion. Yet they are not illusions. They
are real: because the poetic of all our languages has the more potential
for concretion. It can be said that either these poems recognize their
suspension so clearly, concretize their suspension so clearly, or from
their suspension recognize their ground so clearly that the glare
(regularity/clarity) of that vision has created a solid about itself such
that chaos is the only ground.

Mr. Roberson,
from the Preface
to The Next Song

seven songs of loss before the next song

1

you will not be even once allowed
to erase   exactness is your eyes
what you cannot see do not record
as none   any mistakes in size
of said must stand as where you are

2

this is the first elimination.
this is the largest elimination
not for the loss at this point
but many are lost here after all
of the other graces are centered
and this is the point.
they are lost here
and now.   all those
who answered pharoah —
                    or cherokee . . . . .

3

this is nostalgia othellonot grace.
you were not sold a ticket home
from italy why
shld you mourn a true grace
your monkey suit was not on that titanic
why shld you weep
you come from   a better coming you know
I can tell you   this is about the judgement   now
that it is time to speak the language
at hand   that you have lost the came wch
leaves   you free to have the proper moons
you will not be even once allowed
to erase

4

there is nothing you have not
already been exposed to
some in different states
at the various reigns of heat
"A kind of witch doctor told us that a name is the same name
that has a property."
today the addresses of hydrogen
open the zoo
ological gardens of ologicals
upon you this is less than nothing
some indifferent states

5

history and chauvinisme
art and the functioning gentleman
scientiful thought and the nigger calling called.
the losses.
wch brings us to metaphysical hope
beautiful evidence of even the most ordained
physical evidence of even the most insane
in/the way   they come/from   they stand
one hand in death and in the other life

6

you live in the pan who are maligned with balance
you live the wgt whose counter lies   off fulcruming.
in the light against darkness you never light the cross
your face the sun of night   what you cannot see.
in the cutting off of hands you never left the body
your left hand is black   do not record as none.
any mistakes in size   you fit
the physical evidence of even the most insane
them or me bang

7

you
look around you look how many of you
how many deaths you have died
that have brought you to life.

fear is fear that the first death
impresses itself too long
on the water
        on the rest
        of this I must ride

on the water
you must let me ride   I know it

from ETAI-EKEN (1975)

Dani Word Song

etai.
AY-tai.
singing
i.e.,
victory dance.

etai-eken.
AY-tai AY-ken.
seed of singing
i.e.,
soul.

i.e.,
soul .

Ankh

aku'aba

Formula for the Poem Dance

                    turn ambiguity
                    into separation
                    separation into repetition
        turn   repetition into chant
        turn

        The poem for the movement

                    the rock
                    in the rapids glazed
                    with a wave of ice
                    cold water

                    is it there
                    isn't there

                    a place
                    in a movement stayed
                    with   a pin of point
                    in the move

when you are   your nervous system
when you are   potted in your brain
in   your body
    your world   potted in the earth
    to look out   of your mind
    to look into   your works
        to look at
          to look   blossom
          out into (at
          the same time)
      your world (is   fragrance
            seeing   is   your breath
                one time

[33]

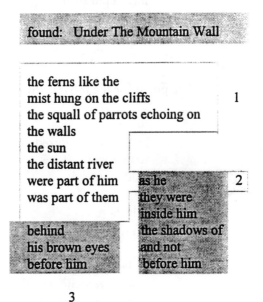

the ferns like the
mist hung on the cliffs   1
the squall of parrots echoing on
the walls
the sun
the distant river
were part of him   as he   2
was part of them   they were
                              inside him
behind   the shadows of
his brown eyes   and not
before him   before him

                    3

pg. 4
Under The Mountain Wall
Peter Matthiessen

[34]

. . .

1 at having seen   there was great stillness
2   like sight placed
3 everything in place was a first thing
4   the note of seeing the mark of sight:

at having seen   there was great stillness.
spotted days go still at his sight.
need was all that grew move
that left a sign   behind   how to get
to it   that was as his as his stomach
and returned him a great stillness.

cities were unheard of
as he is   as one with the center   he comes as he goes
gather-less   migrationless.
death he has not heard of
as he is   as one of its stomach   he would return
an ungrowling great stillness.

the smoke of the insects over the hot fields hangs.
the growing hangs   up to the sky
where his wife has pinned it to the earth.
what is theirs goes still at his sight
the moment   he sees   his wife sees
him   home   she   hangs in the air

her hand
there was great listening
which was the music

the moment him home   he sees she
he sees she
his wife sees hangs in the air
hangs in the air

there
was great listening
which was the music

. . .

2   like sight placed
    always before my sound
    seeking you.

    a bird is its name
    its call is/
    its place is   its sight like you.

    but today in your answer order
    is no stillness
    it is my breaking

    my neck to get to you
    when i see you   i tie order
    with the veins of my neck and spit

    its yelling what it is to see you
    on you   like a net
    the first song.

    like a bird is its name its call is
    you are in your place that is you.
    but there more.   and it takes more to place you
    than naming in place makes go still.

    i am calling things other than their seeing names
    i am other than seeing things i call
    this place   against wch only what i need moves   off
    i am moving

    my feet are in more footsteps than walking   for you
    all i've ever taken are exhausted.
    i am using others'.   then the living's are exhausted.
    the dead's have a move again.

[37]

the million shapes hidden in one run thru each other
the one shape of every nature feeds thru itself
the jaguars and the sun and trees are brothers
passing thru each other's spots til a coat is knotted

exchanging   is a new scale color feather light on them
and a new sister   on them
what is this new   sweat glowed one called dancing
this stillness move lives in called music   that is you?

. . .

3   everything in place was a first thing
    part of him as he was part.
    inside   behind him his eyes.
    seeing was a first thing.
    his stomach bore

    to light
    his male third leg its little eye and two
    reversed stomachs bore

    outline
    the exacted in   everything in place

    with the lightning
    of a move.
    move was a hidden first thing.

    move lit from stillness
    (lightning   and thunder
    making a break for it
    sounds out stillness from deep
    in a first thing as shape

    he can eat he can take
    home for his
    walls   his floors
    or knot the veins of his neck as
    fed as   a song like   a breastplate
                                a body

. . .

4 the note of seeing   the mark of sight
                    sounds out stillness
                        as a shape.
                      a secret name
          of all the colors of an earth as your skin
              drum   painting
                      is brown

          as. you.   light in it body.
                there are no words to
        the sound but when pressed as to meaning
                    we are one
                    (meaning

... *When Everyone Is Beauty is a Time Of Day in Zulu*

you say beauty in my language
by saying a color
it is the color of a time of day.

in the light of a certain time of day
is when everyone is beauty.

when the sun setting
makes you look at everything it's on
like looking on a young girl the instant she becomes

who we also call a color
it is a color called   fresh puddle in the gully:

when a small rain in the afternoon like a dawn
leaves a small golden face mirror in the clay
for a girl to wake up in

to the color
of her small breasts   the color of clay
                             in the clay colored water
                             in the clay

you say beauty in my language
by saying a color   and everyone is beauty
is that time of light

        when the sun makes us see on everyone
        the color of our first girl we all come from.

just before the bed
of the day
into night.

Nature Poem

your nervous system
potted in your brain
your body
potted in the earth
of your mind
your works
blossom
your breath
fragrance

A hammer is always brought to the building
And building over
Years of living have to simplify
to tell us what to do with the house.

Immediate as touched   what to do with a hammer
is nailed to our hand
Our houses are not ourselves as our hammer is our hand
Tho we've lived as long as we've built to live

. . . Longer
Touch as handle   fits the hammer more than
the particular hand
And men and living longer than particular man.

Certain old things are things we always have our hands on
and certain things like their way we always have on our hands.

There is a way you can draw
a bird by putting two wing lines
on an x

wch is place
wch is up   on a pole as a
          cross
between place and moving.
it will look
like an E
of trailing feathers and tail
off a pole   head   in a direction

you can use the hawk as
the floor plan

the shape of the work/day/earth
                    I worked
was an E   of the 17 th
                floor
when I worked at an ad agency.

that high i
could use the birds outside

the window as floor plan

elevators scream in tall old buildings
as though they feel their open shafts
as we do.

a possession.
gods riding them.

on the table I can hear coming
the greensburg account drawings
like the 4 o'clock messenger

we have to get them out for

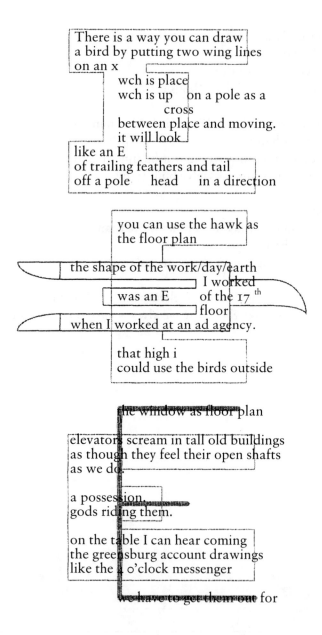

. . .

drawing this way hold of you
all the lines you know supposed
to go to infinity do

with something on them
from your desk

in the studio
my drawing table was

at a window at the back
of one of two airshaft
light wells formed by two
of three wings off the back
of the main bldg
i drew facing this
window   see   my back
to the door

with my arms flat out
up the ramped parallels of the drawing
table sighted thru the posts of the window
up between the wings   the air
shaft   of the light
well   into the sky
my desk went.
out the window

the mathematik concentration of the body
in a line of the pyramids as   a vanishing
point in a road
distance in the prayer of drawing

comes to me

[45]

as why
     my control
     my panel in front of me
     my work is very exact
it is not about the greensburg savings thing account.

. . .

it must be that in the midst
of any tonal language
there is a constant huddle
of all substances' matters

where any accident of sound
could speak and
the sound of people's walk
talk   chicken with your head pecked

is their baldhead heels
in the midst of a song another
song   and any doing sing its work
song

if i must think i must think
i must think well

this is to demonstrate
i must think
my meanings are tonal

the bell ringing
from the well

in the line i must think
it is tonal
i must think well

it is tonal   too/ much
as this is rhythm

        walk talk chicken wid yo head pecked
        you cn crow w'en youse been dead
        walk talk chicken wid yo head pecked
        you cn hol' high yo bloody head
like

[47]

we haven't lost much   (language
but not music as
speaking the drummer walking on   (or
his hands

. . .

the thousand legged foul to sweet
smelling poisonous millipede
            the street
the street   step for step walks on
like on a mirror
            dances underneath him.
the steps are not that clear
but the dance is
            for his sweet life
and he knows the pass-through   corner
he's lined up to.

the traffic backed up from center
and kirkpatrick st. keeps step
            hung
out   talkin into the crowd like bent
down   yellin into the cars from a curb
            speed.
overhead   third to third
floor over the street's top down
            radio up
loud   out ridin   they hang over the sills
and high ride the caller's   yell over the dance.

and at that corner five streets come down
from over the hills to be   made one
            high breaking still.
what one car radio has on when it gets there
every open window has in it
            and every tenant
in the living surface of
that station is poppin to it
            back
of what they do   the stinging
hit they get on it   keep the millipede in shoes
    . . .

[49]

. . .

the zebra is two
animals crossing through
themselves at one
time
how many legs
how many ever
heads at one
time you see their two
colors
the jaguars and the sun
and trees are brothers
passing through each other
in their coats
hunting for some disease in a joseph's

any moment   (12/4/69   4:30 a.m.   chicago

the open door and oh no
and the wish it wasn't
murdered in its sleep
its wife and soon baby
thrown by the police
into your turn
to see the maybe
home open the door oh no

[51]

. . .

how many ever
heads at one
time you see their two
colors

the jaguars and the sun
and trees are brothers
passing through each other
in their coats

walls and the spots
bleeding down the plaster and the night
they were shot are panthers
passing through their brothers
in the skin

... *The Nature Poem*

the yellow pencil rolls across the orange table
into the red shadow
of the sun through the window.
the empty house does not look

like all the flying it has done.
the moves of my re entry
fool the pattern
               of the shot
firing in the turning of the earth.

i am quick and i move
the yellow pencil from exactly where
i left it   its line on the lever
edge of the shadow   lowering
the sun on the nation.

this is a nature poem for black panthers
this is the yellow old eye
of watching   right with seeing
turning the nature of the vision red for you.

. . .

they are crazy and crazy
is as their way   as ours
                    is ours
and that   is how they are
                    that
which we all are one
of / that is   god

and that in our respect
was our mistake
to take them as gods because
we were

it was right but
it was only right

they were something else

Ate'be Tiawu'nanu'

"My children, when at first I liked the whites,
 My children, when at first I liked the whites,
 I gave them fruits,
 I gave them fruits."
                    Left Hand, chief of the southern Arapaho

Ni'-athu'-a-u' A'haka'nith'ii

"I'yehe'! my children — Uhi'yeye'heye'!
I'yehe'! my children — Uhi'yeye'heye'!
I'yehe'! we have rendered them desolate — Eye'ae'yuhe'yu!
I'yehe'! we have rendered them desolate — Eye'ae'yuhe'yu!
The whites are crazy — Ahe'yuhe'yu!"

"In this song the father tells his children of the desolation, in consequence of their folly and injustice, that would come upon the whites when they will be left alone upon the old world ... "

The Ghost Dance Religion and the Sioux Outbreak of 1890,
James Mooney

[55]

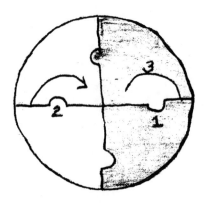

A-nea'thibiwa'hana

"The place where crying begins,
the place where crying begins —
The thi'aya,
The thi'aya."

"In preparing the sweat-lodge a small hole, perhaps a foot deep, is
dug out in the center of the floor space, to serve as a receptacle for the
heated stones over which the water is poured to produce the steam.
The earth thus dug out is piled in a small hillock a few feet in front of
the entrance to the sweat lodge, which always faces to the east. This
small mound is called thi'aya in the Arapaho language, the same name
being applied to a memorial stone heap or to a stone monument. . . .
The thi'aya is mentioned in several of the Ghost-dance songs, and
usually, as here, in connection with crying or lamentation, as though
the sight of these things in the trance vision brings up sad
recollections."

The Ghost Dance Religion and the Sioux Outbreak of 1890,
James Mooney

. . . (word

it has turned over
on my own road
on my own foot
my own way of living
what on earth is the matter with me

the place where crying begins
the place where crying begins
it is the inside
heaped outside   mountain
over wch we step to get in

place where am
place where is   skin
place where sweat and shaking
crying begin
the place where crying begins

. . .

       beasts   dogs   the bitter water
       in their faces
they sat down where they were brought to
a stop   on the beach of the slave coast
       on the sidewalk
surrounded   waiting to be loaded aboard
       the ship and the paddywagon
                to be taken to
       the block and the jailblock
             deeper and deeper
       into the west
when they started singing

the trader and the cop asked
       what were they singing   in what tongue
       what they had to sing about
someone reported
       they were singing about
       their return as killers of their killers
       their return as the freedom
       the free keep themselves from
       by keeping freedom from them

       as killers of their killers
       and about the end of it

       o freedom   about the end of it

. . .

many made no sound when they were murdered
it was long and took a life
time like a move made over a long time
no one notices   the earth's goosebumps
the mountainous
stand on end of horror on the dark skin
many died so deep
the grand eternal moves of that level
met this speck and skidded through infinities
a startled carcass
whole systems too late for the surprise

i have seen
rubber armed
junkies of this stretching
after them
i have seen the far out
almost reach clear
to them   i have made
something to take
from the scabs
on my eyes from what i've taken

to them.

. . .

you see it clearly
then you have to
deal with did you
to yourself
you have to
then come to grip
with honesty
wch is continuing to see
clearly   you have to fight
what you won and lose
not let
honesty win but honestly
lose

. . .

the killed appear to the killer
clear about the weight of the damage
to be carried together
by clearly not being there to help.
their face in all the faces of survivors
whose memories are maimed or carry nothing
have a clear and final say.

this is how our pickings face appears to white people.
clearly black.
and this is how their bone faces appear to us
who clear and calmly
this time turn our back   to understand.
that clearly white.

. . .

the worst disappointment
was we were technicians.
the crazy men invented
knowledges to cure themselves
and were holy.

the priests we were going to be
hated them as we didn't
in our envy.

the worst disappointment
was we knew how
about nothing more than how.

the dumb knew it
who were made dumb by it
and were gifted and silent.

the worst disappointment
was we were ourselves
and the others of ourselves who were each
other made a mountain
impossible for us alone to scale.

the one we were going to
be left out by definition.

the worst disappointment
was we were wise in only wisdom
like those before us
letting our brother unknown
let us in his silence
make fools of ourselves.

the knowledge we were going to be

the light   not as sure
as the simple dark people are
that they are true.

. . .

it's put these days that
european culture appeared at
other peoples' cultures at the vulnerable time
of lowest energy or decay   (or
                that mexico city was sinking)

it hasn't been put yet
that our energies are world wide that world
culture was at
a same point and the acts of the europeans

were their own
weakness
and all this their mold
they have always fit as breakers down

from the the high cheeses of reason
to rotters.
and it hasn't been put
that that too had its point and vulnerable

time in america

and that black culture stood for
always ready for the least

sign of montezuma's weakness
in white guts toward their culture
to give them its traveling music and to teach
them to dance well

. . .

american culture   is the pot
calling the skillet black. american
even as a mulattoed
culture is very deeply colored. folks

white america is an unconscious black
brother culturally to black americans
as though still in a blanched coma
from the burn

that

chuck berry's
elvis presley charlie mc carthy
was actually
a dummy.
it said what he said
and made you move your head
yes

that
nigger is the man.

even black people had to
read it in translation to be sure
it was that hot a star they saw
the wise men coming
toward
themselves.   had to read its
hips
because in europe they don't talk that.
not 'til turkey
at least.

. . .

... *Wave*

everyone sees the sea coming down the beach
everyone calls it the white horses.
nobody's language is ever mistaken
they never fail to come called
on any shore they are broken to.
there is a man who has seen the distance
in the desert do just that
same break   at a walk.
he calls the horizon the white horses
and i have called my sight the reef.

i can imagine that black men call them
the white dogs
and that for the same reasons
the earth could come to call the spray
stars of the milky way
the middle passage
coming down the black sand space
like it was as due as justice
a simple wave   landing and
towing the blanched shell it has taken back like slaves.

. . . once

thinking the hummingbird
the calligraphy
of an eastern language
sent between bright flowers,

he sat and applied
to the school of their hand,
the sun at its head.
the written reply came in his own

days.

the only erasures were the nebulae
not the nights.
night couldn't make written
remove not blank

and not there like distance
could.
he applied for right the first time
as his own hand.

yes took the lifetime he lived on no to come.

light took the lifetime he lived in the dark
to arrive at him.
the obscurity was clarity that late
illumination couldn't cover

nor make
a having known where to look
before the star appeared as clear
as his skin

could. there all the time, his hand.

writing in a right the first time
hand   he was darker
in the light than even in the dark.
he could not repeat

and that was accuracy
that was hand
grown beauty   the erasure
the nebulaic smear of the dark that is

light shows him up dark print   bird on his dark background.

. . . a black man's black is his mysteries

a black man's black
face and his black heart
when they're pure
are not not white
nor are they white.

a black man's black
or white is right
in his face
in the blindness of that wch goes around
coming around.

a black man's black
as night is day around
itself
is likewise one
that resolves the many in the one, too.

... *The Mojo Against Genocide Was Taken Care Of In The Beginning*

there is a hole in a shadow
through it a blinding light shines.
it is the eye of a shadow)
and that is why
you can't see it
every shadow is the dark
person   the earth will never be bare of
black people

as long as the sun shines.
the sun makes us
this way
as long as the sun keeps
you alive   it will make
black people.
when you do not need the sun
peoples you will not need yourself

. . .

the music someone has put on
walks him through the streets.
he never lets its feet touch the ground.
it receives the honored meat
behind the breastbone at the sound
of its drum.   drum for drum.

it takes the rhythm no one is without.
its heart is strengthened
until no one is without its heart.
no one is without the buried rag he bends
into the earth to bring up and take out
the ancient blood egg the testicle part

himself reclaimed and part his won
gift his peoples feeds his soul on.

from LUCID INTERVAL AS INTEGRAL MUSIC (1985)

Picking Up the Tune, the Universe and Planets

this form is the lena
after my daughter
here she is I will have to
hold   on a minute tell you her line.

a scribble
the universe and planets holes and scribbles
pure
interruption she gets   her changing

she is the only music   she gives
the intervals
in which it is written.
she is

back she only wanted me to pick her up to say so.

I. still autonomic
still as

[72]

I.   still autonomic
               still as unspected as conception's
                      about what now-breathed message
reflection prior to its face
          should carry on

                            at seeing.

about what you claim as
          —If I am the lake you take your face from—
a reflection
at the sight of me,
                  I crawled

as far back in as I could to you
          into the water's trouble,

          into yet templet noise
              between each word,
inchoate sea that spirals as shell does out
          —helpless as any later meanings—
as the world.
                  The father has

always been brought to his knees
          by this.

[73]

fear that
the terror the peter pulled out short of

bearing, always tricked, had this
time also got through,

that twin, the disorder, stowaway again,
had, with won life, reset all's possible end,

and that fathers, held to more than
their power   songs now cover,

have to re-face
          meaninglessness,

clutching infants who
          haven't yet words,

screaming for them
                    their protective songs
          incoherently.

I.

because the final
confessions of a coarse air
bail the fire out
we are innocent of adduction.

taking the body down
we thought was a solo for fuel.
shoving it in for warmth
we cracked

our perpetual jar of things
to a more
naked jarring blast.
The crimes wch you wear my body for

I myself committed.

II.

songs without words
scenes of infants.
or o sing unto the lord
good morning as birds.

tribute to the saintly
the bait   the killers.
endangered animals
will they survive? this is all.

the perpetual jar of things
i don't know where
from   it's caused   or filled
or quoted without these words

I am shaken.

---

2.   I might have screamed
           the wrong spell, the wrong words,
the wrong defiance thrown the property
          against the specie for,
for love
          written a senseless draft and wasted
myself at war, like my age,
          remembering the more complete
for bottoming out of means
          human
to even sit down and eat beside another
          to ride on a bus or go to school
to recall any chance at all of an even
          hand   free of the holding
                    class

III.

the rice care
is left in the frog harp.
several early songs
hurt the farmers' heart

after nightfall.
to mention the soldiers
is to state it to death.
a souvenir silence.

string in a labyrinth.
no giving away
is the look out
commanding the entire face

floating without bottom in that earth

---

remembering the more complete
        the more the perpetual
jar of things
        lends no aright,   nor tapped,
no center on the wheel. all form, all voice
        is clay. in different. we
are right only
        to what we give birth to, anyhow,
we are correct only within
        what we create,
only
        the examinations we make
up out of each
        last hour's erasures mark us right.

IV.

The park geese
are dozing at their dance
on water.
Their necks

in the straps of their closed wings
They are swung like subway riders
depicting the floating
carcass

is a high form of held
Instant in dance
As fleet as death is in life.
The river stone is here

A black step in a tree reflection skipped still.

---

4.   because of the suggestion all the versions
                    of peoples in trees make
        to americans,
                the africans, the pater monkey, the
                        jesuses crucified, the lynchings
        the yearbook blondes swung in
                all the alumni arbors,

        the surface of the water reflects what is
                Under the umbrella of such leaves
                        Even stone leaps to the surface
        The stones on the bottom are mistaken for the bottom
                of a hanging
                        black man's feet on the surface
        reflection. Dancing nationally in the trees or.
        A skipping stone. Also skipped still strange fruit

V.

A sudden smoothness like a glass
between the swells   enchanted valley
wandering the wild sea drifts.
The cloud deer cross the road,

the main shipping lanes,
searching after it   in the snow
it is that master
flake of all possible design

when compared in size.   the pin
of the spin of the ocean.
of all migration
The course of the target

only   makes all the objects.

---

5.   You can stand in a field at night and hear the snows land.
     The ton of an instant's impacts taken all but one,

and a sea cleared in silence for that's star:
and seas of the mirror moon

that radiant from, say, one crater
taxiing to time as copernicus.

That flake.
That sound.

The beacons, the landing lights strike me as spinal,
as physical shivers

the silence in which this traffic fields
its tar baby.

[79]

VI.

there are no stars in
the metropolitan
area skies
only air traffic.

Twenty-one landing
lights. Call
that mobile
the constellation Holding

Pattern, a modern
form in time
enough to save our navigation
of a maintained

in the nebulaic   escape of bearing from here.

VII.

With the dead rest
spots in the oscillation
an accuracy also,
a perfect note is

hit. An accurate physical absence.
The presence of music.
Or conversation
with one

I think is never missing
and I think is the right signature.
To have squandered an intelligence
on unspeakable watch

of that   without tongue

VIII.

the cobra standing
drops down to strike
like   the tabled elbow rolls the arm
down to the mark of the hand.

on the stairs
of the snake's crooked back
the fangs hang out
on the landing.

whoever's on the floor tonight
his chin on the concrete
will spot their scale as the last
conscious credential handed out

not any manipulation near to a signature.

---

8.   In mesoamerica the snake's head touches
      down to the ground. You are bitten
             by birth. It isn't a trick.
You start
    dying. How can anything kill
        you ascending the steps
to the hour-
    fanned feathers of skies?

Our pyramid   is we've perfected
    not being caught,
        throwing folk skyward through the stories
of structures absently
    as hope, elevators we prescribe in the voice
        of those who stand watching

IX.

we can run out of our side
streets like out our ribs
between the buildings of owner
abandoned meat   to see the dead star.

we can bleed as really as
humanly possible and prove nothing.
raise no more of the dead than good has
in our lifetimes.   lying in the streets

are stars while their perfect point in shining
on the books without meaning to be fixed upon.
secrets   which orbit decent decision
so distant from anywhere   real

seeing to it it is only in our stars

X.

blood: someone says it's not
red until it runs
up and touches the air
loose.

it probably has the light
on different
inside and can cross on the knife
suddenly appearing through

appearance not even as particular as street
the thought of.   the light changes
passing through limitations
like human skin: candlelight thru fingers or yellow

vision the distress symptom of rattlesnake bite.

XXII.

We had seen a first
Lady haul ass
over the trunk of
the assassination car

faster than split
second's
photography could catch. it
Looking for the spirit

leaving the body
We. find character.
acting to refer
our scramble over our dead

to a common class. not exactly a pieta position
on all fours, bookin'

XXXVII.

The notebooks are where the foot
soldiers are buried beneath
where the war is won.
A lot of this mind

is the flower yard you will have
to go down among and find
gone.
You are not kept up either.

Grave out of which inspiration were
to raise
your figure is cast on that very field
ground reverse and lives are opinion

changes which do not occur in space.

Interval And Final Day's Concerts

III.

knowing the music
      never comes into
               it.
the music's fact is
      a glossolalia
           sound's meaning.

record jacket
      -cover art's point
           cuts its own
      music
different from that
      the magnetic pick-up
             fit is on.

Point in these words
      takes up the turning
           subject
after the silence after
      what was meant last.
   At renewal.
A needle
      not so played on meaning
           as on moving
rescue   from blank death
      death's and other words' subject
             radical.
     As many names
for the same deck as games,
      as human call is
          figurature
upon those acids.
          And once in person,

[87]

from VOICES CAST OUT TO TALK US IN (1995)

Chapter One,
I. Aerialist Narrative

Written into   the drip accomplished
form   of action painting   the lyric
for people who walk on strings

There are photos of people standing
on the canvas
in mid-air   a line ahead of the painting.

Of what happens,
lines of that   are gone,
not simply missing

Those lines of how those
lines that are there   got there
the line in mid-air

from the can to the surface
its moment like a line written
in that falling hand of the northern lights.

But what can anyone have read,
supposing it was night,
by the light of Icarus or any of us escaping?

II. Taking the Print

See night in the sunlight's starry reflection
off the water   darkening the water
by contrast.
                    The dark hiding in the water
also hid us in the river at night
Our crossing guided by the internal sight
on our darkness
                         the ancient graphis
and — from this passage of abductions and escapes —
this newer imprimatur of the river
cut deep in the plate.
                                   see in the river the ripples'
picture on the surface of the wind the lifting of the image
has taken at the deeper face
                              the starry freedom
written in the milky rivery line that pours
the brilliance of that image from a depth only black
night fleeing across this land
                                   has to voice.

III. Heading: The Landing

The beacon fires   the hidden fears;
the runway lights,   their nature's lies,
the country's lies:

will arrival even be any
base left to touch
once these few minutes run out
their approach?

Is a way in air   so clear and orderly
as the light is,
drawn as a landing about the ground?

Voice closest to closure of the journeying
is one that deserts us,   the one called silence,
leaning in the glass against its image,
as if all diagram is a delusion of process.

All these voices come out to meet us in this
ancient seeing in the end of distances
this fearing:
the glow of the coming city
on the horizon   is it burning;
is this music or screaming
all these voices cast out to talk us in?

What if in the final
minutes of your heavying
descending

the landing strip kept lying
changing you back
into the air   the way a white

backs away in anger when you approach with the directions
you've been asked?

[90]

In like manner the entire society remains
up in the air   black unaffirmed mirage
a mountainous range   teetering on its own
upside down
peak denying what it's risen of.

Solid rock lifting itself into the air
on its own heated reflection   illusions of separation
that anyone trying
to place down   to integrate into   goes also up
in the confusion.

Ours is a particularly hard landing always
trying to correct to an abandoned position
You run out of the fuel for holding
back

the fires of arrival

the few survivors
those who packed to die
maybe raised

like images
of smoke
slapping our faces with our color

a wafer from the stack
of all our waiting number

a cup snatched
before the take too much
to

A kind of conclusion
that's cleared away.   Like wreck or sin.

V. Properties

After some days —
    and not because of the dirt —
it really looked
    like a kind of earth
and not the fallen sky it had been at first
    snow.

Whether the vengeful one
    were the ground or the sun —
then, whether thats
    stamp or kiss were a crash or press
into that print
    an attempt coins on survival,

— commemorative myth
    the spun tales of these genes —
whatever,   ours, like water's
    is not material fatigue.
Up and down time after time
    how many migrations
has ice made home
    to water?

The verdant tropical mists' drip
    tears   gathering into the cold
bloody rivers of the atlantic
    grinding ashore
captured into the plantations' white glacial field
    the rending melt water's burst
toward a north star   state to state
    of matter

pressed upon us
    our material does not fail
the strict coinage   It would be different
    if the investigation team had overlooked
a piece of the wreckage in the staring face
    of Icarus

Black with the road's dusts,
    the atmosphere,   solid, on the ground
turns into a pool, the
    ground's mirror,
and picks up the sky again.

IX. The Motorcycle Crossing

1

Sometimes it's all in
      how you get seated
            in the road of the morning   This morning

I was sitting right
      at the desk kicking out
            paper like miles

and like coming up over the top of a hill
      into sun   or air   or clear
           of the high road roar

I laid her over right there.

2

You don't think   you run over them
       and snakes can rope up
           into your spokes
and throw the bike.

       It takes nothing,   a stone.
          So ain't nothin happenin
in the office   and you lay it down
       mean it
          all going down inside.

Secretary step in   you
       sitting at the desk   unannounced a
          silver veil of tear weaving down

your face   a landscape
       singing quiet to yourself
          Every little thing
Gonna be alright.

No snake   no slick   no stone
I just laid it down.

3

               Late afternoon summer
the long rhythm of soft running
       water and its silence,
           you could hear the wake of the collards
parting the water.
       The long black lines,
           her fingers, passing through.

When we were growing up   you know
       those sisters at the sink
           in the kitchens baptizing those greens
suddenly break
       down into tears   jump up singing
           shout
Don't worry
       Don't worry   some day
           It a be alright

4

must be in my blood
       blood my blood

           has had to lie in
absorbing the lives
       we were losing   bathing in screams

       The tide rhythm blood
and filth took on
       rocking in that deluge
           those ships cupped to our god for drink
must be in my blood

Given our own blood to drink
                    Bloods of the hold
Bloods of the fields
            drying in those furrows
                    through our feet

as up through any root
            blossoming at the tip
                    of our touch into the cloud
boll   held an instant then sacked
            the bitterness of this fruit
                    clothing a nation

leaving for work this morning
            in new blood   a new press
                    the rungs on the upward ladder
treacherous
            as the deepened sea.

XI. Given Way
(to Tom Mellers)

Flying isn't always that best
      you can do left
behind, that over and above
      spoken of.

Sometime you have to return over
    the river   as the limo driver
      after having

seen off a burden of chastening
      envies from JFK,
      have to,

though driving,   passenger a sleek
      abandonment,
and lightened to nothing of your claims
      have to

drop your gloves as though a will
      from the wheel,
drop the rein that points the way less
      than the barn itself,   the throttle

less than place in tight formation
      taking us on in
             flying

Not that transcendence,   not a grace;
      though, like it,
no choice, an automatic
      pilot

how it follows the road has brought
      us to the bridge
on the fly of crossing and not
      the stop of jumpstreet
off.

                And if,
as you say, Jessye Norman   was singing
                Jerusalem
at that instant and the structure

                of the bridge,   in crossing,
painted trusses of Franz Kline blackouts
            on   the lighted city,

                        flying is only
how you've seen what you had to
            stand on
and not had way
                        to look.

Chapter Two
IV.

        The skipping stone stays out of the water
The standing up in the boat crossing
the delaware,
the band-aid commercial parade
of drum, flag and fife,   the iwo jima
collection, things that are terms like
four little girls flying

        around inside an exploding church,   people
being washed down
the street with water,
dogs in the saint george and the dragon
art history position
on command on top of women
the camera catches,   the skipping stone

        stays out of the water
long enough to cross over
concurrence   to accountable term
but not over   the deaths of those who go
under   say just prior the altared shore
who are entire now.   complete,   not ideal.

        A prediction of that bird iridescence,
the spot of a single reptilian scale,
is passed without going the full length,
to one down the sequence   suddenly
across the looped catastrophic
plane of locomotion.

Tossed off on blank sand,
the line   in a sidewinder's hand
explaining lifting off the continuum
of the earth,   explaining leaving one surface
for another   to arrive elsewhere
on the first   in time

to take up the percussion of living
on the one hand and have to
strike death into its dance down the other,
any distance between   coiled tightly
around the rattling emptiness   to drive a sense
like that gourd's hidden singing   of beaten time

from inside   secret   singing
to fly the round walled ground the seeds throw
like bones   the steps   our coiling hips
our music   leaping off
this plain like light a dance
that forward takes us higher

How if stepping skips those places
how then dancing flies.   how
matter admitted and explained lifts from its lie
its term of flight accountable to be done
something with   a stone touched down to resurrect
prediction to a dictate
to organize our missing   and from that ghost create

      those backs of the waters
we cross upon.   those black shadows no
that black apotheosis
in the simples shared indigenous american things.
already.   an Osiris
the middle passage has brought home along
what rivers deltas and mississipis mean to U.S.

      But this is what is always skipped
this is the lift the country gets to get
moving   the term
mickey mouse renewed each generation
evokes your hugs   What face stirs your concern
like one of color except   to lemming separation, to out-
      distance
      is renewed

IX.

           The birds put inside·
    what the walking felt divide
         their going,

    what — without that void,
         the ground between step —
  brings walking to its cul-de-sac.

    The birds put nothing in their bones

In their bones
     how nothing frees them   how nothing lifts

them up   What your own
     people never wanted you to have to know

and feel sorry for you if you don't
     takes you to the river told you

wash away your   tears   wash away
     your tears   are the rivers and even they will

wash away

I was afraid
     I find out what it mean
         it a be alright

what it mean what it   meano
     mean   it mean
         it won't no and it won't

matter at some point
     even that
         be alright

Chapter Three
VIII. Ask for "How High the Moon"
(for Nathaniel Mackey)

a half moon at midday,
if you've seen
    the gelatinous medusa

you know how it looks
    like it leans
its jelly umbrella and melt-off fringes
    into the wave   and wind
        of sunlight

The organism's membranous
    delicacy, a silk stinging
        thing like beauty
carried above beauty   carried away
    the sky its

        pale parasol borealis
the bride a gauzed nubian shadow
        moon holding   carried away
damask balloon torn in two
    over itself.

    Such as yourself
        say,
    living down to what

    means
the melt pools in the market lot reflecting

    a sky
    the ended days of freeze
have glaciered liquid flawless

                    can afford
              for looking up . . .
                    Leaving the store

I overheard somebody say
        "Look, the full moon,"
                    at only the half

carried away up.
              And down time after time,
                    how many migrations
has ice made home
              to water?   And winters, to this spring?

the light and shadow holding together.

                    *

              If in
        the very pool you're looking
down into to look up   at the moon
                    out of   out of
it is thrown at you   a stone
              from the tire
        of a car plowing through it
                    the turning

              seasons' wheel   Or
        there appeared
        on your forehead
        this stone that backwards
threw down   into the water's trouble

of turning and tire   that arrow
        of time which film reverses
              stilling the waters   Then
        see the hard thought at the bottom
weighting the reflection of its moon

                    [104]

creation   loss
each distinguished from our ghosts

           *

Sculpted out of the sun-polished snow
the small david of a puddle

out of how stone can sling up at you
if you're looking   (arrowheads   the moon

ignescent associations between things:
the cold star struck from the broad day.   Light.

When Ailey set it
to music Billie got knocked down to

what a little moonlight can do
the white stuff of cost

danced   to music ask
for How High the Moon   and you want

Ella to sing it   bring it down
like that time she admits   carried away in time

she can't remember the words to this
but what she does in time

is
greater song the rest us

jus mostly cries out
no forward no back

[105]

＊

hit in the head by the moon
no one can take the stone of that light

out of your human skull
no one can tell

where the bone and the sight
actually separate

                      now
the lost sight of all gap
opening on that

nothing they put in   their bones

   ＊

the light at midway up
      out of the darkness
           orpheus

all you persephones   you lazari
      christians and other
          resurrectionists

is that circle of listening
      decided
          to tear you apart

I mean this song
     this stone warts
         to dance with you

from ATMOSPHERE CONDITIONS

I. Atmosphere Conditions

That weather when the glide path to Newark
drops the flights below gray solid slab
counties ahead of the usual time,

a lens of crotchety things that brings the lines'
logos closer for us to read, their yell
louder to our attention who don't care

to turn our aid anymore to their wolf
and fatten their audience, used to it.

That weather when you can't tell whether
what you see is yours, nature's or some curve
a public careering through throws on the wall

objects such as Hiroshima's shadows
or any New York subway art that glows
from that ruin or your own   ignis fatuus.

The lighting sigh of decomposition
over some settlement of the grave blows
that figure of atmosphere we named ghost,

mostly our foolishness cast by this light
against the air the rest of time is gone
from us   It burns into stone only this name

you see. Graffiti   appears only on what
is disappearing   marking the going out.

The wall the state the sainted   toppled shit on,
this signing   spray of their prefiguring star
wandered back as ghost   outlined as fallen

on the pavement sky of heaven   chalks upon
arrival   which mark defaces   which adorns,
a cloud or glory   time flies our object through.

Stars snuff out in the sun   as in the dirt
meteoric rainbow or its tornado
granted   equally hit the ground

gold pot or cash   that plasmic electric
green   they each a storm   seize each their audience
in its tracks with seeing   wish take into air

all you already have with all you want
and twisting   turn the horn's plenty to draining need

becoming true.   This funnel of the light
of day   of that old blues turning at its
twenty-four and a fourth singing   "Needmore

have harm a many man . . ." flattens out
to full horizon   a meteor's cards
out on the ground   It rains on your table.

Your wishes are just atmosphere   conditions
Greeks called them meteors   men made predictions
at the sight on weather   Things in the air

literally   and they believed them written
by inflammable gases   as if rainbows
and shooting stars were all a methane

as if lightning and decay venting were blasts
matter farts back at heaven, it then more

a fore-spite   writing than a prophecy given,
as if that apparition of graffitti raged out
of the order   of time   as of behavior.

So are   the great prophesies graffiti,
grumbles written on great weakenings   crayon
on great endings   the earth   the rainbow's crash.

What more can you see than what it is to
see   'cept the trashed meteorology
of writing on the wall   the thin air

You see the thin air before you   spell out
a holy ghost   promised moisture by temperature,
the weather of its proof star   this glory

these going out get sucked up into
but you can't really see.   a black hole

some speak of as astronomical
but you know as maybe your next breath
against air's wall of mirror   without image

which itself is a mark   a meteor
of absence
  . . .

IX. Squall

If I think of the size I was
      at certain memories,

I could see just at the level
      of the window ledge when I
recall the first time I saw
      pigeons wing-singing,

improvising their horizon
      beat by beat,   their wing
voice,   an exaltation in
      the exercising

          I see now.
If I think of the size I was
      at certain questions asked,

I think   more than I heard it said it's called
      a squall   they are squab
your uncles hunt them   they're, she said,
      good eating . . . "   Like question,

satisfying   I see now,
    getting in focus — as commotion —
those uncertainties,   getting a bead
    — within those shiftinesses of need —
on the visceral
    hunger of wanting to know.

Satisfying to see the felt   Inside
    unresolving   Patterns

almost like eating in their exactness,
    always losing the place
of any full filled with the next
    movement.   The flight,

whether in fascist peristaltic line
    or stampede randomness,
isn't the flip card that fish flash,
    isn't the fluid soap bubble iridescing

pigeon holy ghosts of colors,
    vanishing when they light.
Ours is the brown
    paper bag impossible to fight

our way out of
    and possible to drown
being thrown in   — stepping-stoneless —
    the crossless river.

And pigeons
        not that dove,

They are/ Theirs is   a contested
    flight that hangs /or
possible answers on the surface
    of some internal slugging it out
for direction
    in an invisible sack   of headlong space —

Reminds us
    how unseen ours is   although we feel it,

feel the throwing curve a change
    of direction is   the bottom drop out
the dive   takes and upside down the same
    acceleration of some plan taking off
into the lead   outdistancing
    any steps of our control,

we feel punched
    back into our seats   catching up.

If I think of the size I was
made   by the excitement
      improvised on that horizon,

I see now
      the seat in an amusement   buckled in
the mind   throw me to the ceiling sky,
      side to side,   its swung argument

ages to sport   or dance
      or which least resistance
opens to escape in a riot's panic,
      its roiling perimeters seeking like those birds'

calculations   or hosed back
      down the sky;   in any case, holding
— no matter how snatched or buffeted —
      the form   from within the movement.

I see now.

I stood.   I grew
      the difference in eye level
the squall of differences   of perspective
      of seeings that is,
   collective,
   memory
   the ambiguous undulation
      we work like wing   within
the formation flying of our mind
      that flock of / in
time

[113]

X.   If You Think of the Size

If you think of the size
        you were
                at certain memories,
you would
        hold yourself
                without thinking
now on your lap
        is how you thought
                you'd watch   from the tops of trees
what grown up
        sight sees

hold like a child how
        trains side by side
                floated underground
in different rooms seen
        through the different window speed
                being small
in some one's arms is
        If you think of the change.
                How it all
side by side floats
        in some ground

on a subway yesterday or years ago
        on a night
                train south.
How you'll understand
        as an undergrad the
                popular relativity
explanation model
        from that kid
                kinetic parallax memory
some escape   trick to stay ahead of
        Move that nigger baby

[114]

so's I can sit there or
        I'll get the conductor.
                And not being moved.
Warped years ahead
        through Montgomery-parted
                waters and Birmingham
learning I
        Shall not
                I shall not be moved
and not being moved
        not moved.

. . . . .

The wonder of the movement
        was the feeling
                of being right
of being understood
        As being
                Right
The unity of that
        probably the only
                time we felt
at one
        with this country
                felt to belong
felt not to be opposed
        put out   put down
                put off
we were not outside
        there was no war
                in that warring
moment we
        were in that land and
                in that land the "We
all is one" were free   that land the

Freedom
        we all prayed about

This is a common feeling:
      a commonweal
           we feel
                lost.

XI.   When Change

When change
    came the terror
        they thought
it would hit
    and be over
        with
the worst

a waited out
acclimation;

they never
    thought simply
        change
would change
    into change and
        the always
be

that instead of
something.

                *

It isn't a railroad train
   in an outburst
drumming the tracks
   getting up from

here to there changing
   spots out of
restlessness tonight
   it is the wind

I hear through
   the chimney
as through any
   open

   window horn
put to my ear.

The sea
   has always had
its peace
   through shell to say

how much
   each wave ending
a zero more
   it can't sit still

The hearth's conch
   its breath   curling
an echo of the steam
   engine boogie drumming

   of train track blues
is really attuned   of the heart.

*

That beating has never been cut down

Not through forced relaxation
    of law   nor the deep breaths surfacing
the ghettoes gave   nor the opening
    into stations the body works

That body which by
    having no weight
kept the heart
    rate high

has never been cut down
    swings
at the slightest sound
    into movement

into voice

I hear the have to
    keep moving in the same
ability I have to   see
    Can't see the air for

it telling me   move
    like one by one the trees ditty
bop down the block)
    my black ass

[119]

No longer out of anyone's way
    The way has changed to my way
So I am with it   But I can always
    Tell the wind risin'   leaves

    tremblin' on the trees tremblin'
on the trees

XVII.   Down Break Drum

How a fish might
      look up and
    see the stilt stalker
         heron,

in the West Indian Day
      crowd
    I turn at the
         stilt walker's loud

grand baton foot
      clearing
   a silence
         swept smooth of scared

people backed before
      the bow wave
   its step
         in their noise wakes.

And I am the one
      caught.
   This is what folks talk
         about the gods walking

sitting on your shoulders
      in your shoes
   having consumed
         you

in that beauty

      fixed by
   that crack of the gavel

      your decision made

to face and see.

[121]

XIX.   I Don't See

I expected something up out of the water
not the shadow in the wave that rose

to fill the wave then splash a breath
off the abutting air   then disappear.

I didn't see any of this   only
the dark wave.   Even the size of a whale

I don't see   what I look directly at.
I didn't see the pronghorn antelope,

speed they pointed out equal our car's,
but never having seen distance so large

I couldn't pin in it   point to antler
and saw in parallax instead   the world

entire a still brown arc of leap   so like
a first look at the milky way   each stone

a star I saw but could not see.
I didn't see

the Nazca earth drawings looking at a line
like a path   the vision on it   my not looking up.

& trying to see from on the ground looking
from a plane thousands of feet above

maybe I saw only what the unenlightened
marking out the lines could see from there

because I never saw the figures
until shown from books.

[122]

I've told folk half the truth   that I was there I was
but embarrassed   never told   I missed my chance

until I saw: without embarrassment
this country miss its chance   looking at color

and not see what it looked directly at,
without embarrassment

act   and not see that done
on its own hands   not see its own bright blood.

XX.   I Remember Form

I remember a yellowish color
        suddenly opening in the ground
        just to my left a step ahead
        when I startled a huge adder
I remember the sound it beat
        with its tail in the leaves
I remember the only thing I actually saw
        clearly was the tail withdrawing
        into the muck of the leaves on the jungle floor.

I remember the red brown skin of the porter's
        legs slipping in the mud climbing up
        into the shadows of the overgrowth
        hanging into the deep bed of the stream
I remember the flash of
        red and the machete at the same time
        coming down right behind the heel
        of his own foot and taking off the head
        of the one snake we'd carried
        the antidote against   knowing it is useless

I remember months after being home
        taking off my shirt and pants
        hanging the belt across
        the seat of the chair and the weight of the buckle
        slowly sliding the brown leather down to the floor
I remember jumping naked
        halfway across the room
I remember I did this
        again
        as recent as two weeks ago

The Osiris Addendum

I remember the shock
    of remembering
    that I am
still that   who
    rememberings
    re-member

XXVII.   Corner Stone
(for Jake Milliones

Brick has had this wait before
     how long before
          it's torn
down carrying
     nothing

          weighing in
a coliseum
     grounding out a service
          road   a cobble street
the crushed floor

     the borrowed of the poor
          not our
new idea of environ
     -ment   the other
          continuous

meant by the gleaners'
     beggared pick up
          of the field:
the housing stock
     just sitting

          in the cities   brick and board

droppings of famine
     undigesting bone and
          useless wrapping
the liquid bright
     copper

          ripped out for market.

     *

*

The
copper placed on the scale dish
    to be weighed judged to be worth
        so much baby need
a new pair shoes
    the heart placed
        in the prone Aztec stone man
dish balanced on his stomach
    We place our heart
        on   our poverty
such as god / we
    are nothing
        and it don't mean a thing
the scale still
    motionless
        we are paid.

The collectors
    bag people   hunter-gatherers
        the connoisseurs
yellow leaves or none or few as frame
    -like time
        conspire to put things up.

Or
someone come along & see
    he / maybe / the one fragment
        pick it up
put it in place
    a musician an unsocial
        social architect or

someone tall all legs

[127]

no neck and little
        bad feet
put up a house
        again people can get in
            get off their dogs
& on they own
        We

        have had this wait
before
    (for
        Jake

            *

*

There is that shiver
        up the spine we get we say
                is someone walking on our grave

There is the sense
        we quote of standing on the shoulders
                of giants as though rote

we step only the upward
        But it is in our hands to lay
                what is under our feet

& what makes the distinction
        between being
                walked on and being stood upon

when we see the city
        walking around in his
                works walking in what we have

of now
        if not the golden streets
                Brick

has had this wait before.
        (This is for
                Jake

XXVIII.   Call From Vandall
(for Dick Vandall

The machinery of the air,
        the works
    that never jab up
        into the perceptions,
was caught out
        of some corner of the ear
    floating barely
        above his subliminal,
unmoving   so unlike song.

He'd contacted his senses
        or picked up
    his perception
        before fully leaving
one state
        and so experienced his own

        arrival in another   his eyes opening
          and he was crying.
He often cried in his sleep thereafter.

The crying seems only a part of
        something he was doing
    from the same
        but larger place,
a voice larger than voice is
        here, a heart deeper
    than one could stand for
        in one body
and not be lost as   yet.

Yet he awoke
        wet with it   on his face
    and the sense
        that nothing happened
in the last
        to preclude its being in
    this present.
Only

in different character he feels the same.
The same beings lost, left or killed
            people this,
    people here with some vague sense
        of some history
of passage together
        before   through this
    as if a room   your mother
            walked through before you
arrived.   Then

he felt so many he forgot
and picked up where he was.
            The huge house . . .
the many mansions . . .

XXXIII.   Archaic Song FM

The turning of whatever
          spinning instrument
her time used turned her
          minutes into death

And she would be wound in this
          as in earth
          when her long breath
around the sun completes its skein

and from this fuse
          a fabric of which
mother of silence pieces this
          explosion of starry "O

          I cannot finish" and
"O will it come-o
. . . . My love,
          the metro moves along

a dial   station to station
          None of the faces finishes
its song
          in that window

All of the spinning songs
          we know of
          have no end
The stringy girls thicken into cord

helixing into some next else's
          turn   turning in the beds
themselves instrument
          playing

          out the lines
that knotted   clothe the singing

from WORK IN PROGRESS

Program for The Dance

1.

He turned
    so fast he
        wound
the spirals of his arms
    tight
        into a slap
in the face

    he beat himself to death
        dancing

he would fall
    then get right —
        back up
to some music
    he heard
        all by himself
no one to

    help

        listen

2. *Program*

We tune
    taking in hand
the remote as partner
    to the news.

We turn
    twirling the tit
of the dial   in touch to touch
    between our fingers.

We feel ourselves
    both touch and button
coming on.
    Or is it music we two

pick up step
    to   that times
happening into
    receiving line?

3. *table . . .*

Tied to a table
    top   the table tilted up
       right so
he hung by his ankles,
    he filled from
       a bucket on the floor at his head
the cup at his feet
    overhead   with a spoon,
and when it filled,
then an attendant emptied
    cup back
       into bucket,

and he began again
    doing the senseless   hanging
       sit ups like
prayer   in the morning
    naked,
       his throat cut
draining the words
    into the bucket
       from

which he delivered
    the blood of his songs
       into
the cup of heaven,
    his feet,
       in
steps

4. By The Rivers of . .

The boys came in the house
　　home from day camp
　　　　that summer
they were stopped
　　so many feet into their running
　　　　through the door
made to meet the guests
　　required of　　to sing
　　　　what they had done today
They sang of being taught though
　　they thought they knew
　　　　already how to swim

Asked if they liked it
　　the youngest explained that
　　　　what he liked the best
was to come in
　　through the top door of the water
　　　　into the city
underneath the pool　　He said
　　he saw long lights
　　　　he liked　　people made funny faces
and were flying.

　　I am the guest　　I come in
　　　　through the top door of the water
4 to 12　　for the public
　　aquarium
　　　　I'm a diver
tankman to porpoises,　moray eels,
　　the lightning
　　　　cloud of neon tetras at my hand
I midwife the anaconda
　　— all 60
　　　　plastic wrap egg babies —

[136]

making a living living in a vision
   city
      of living cubes of water

door to door.

Door to door
   tank displays
      on my shift don't get visited
by out of tank appearances
   in their own likeness hiding
      gifts
of transcendence and wisdom
   Rather than glory —
      tubes and cylinders trailing
old air   poor
   disguise flippers for wings
      and gifts no more

than of care and feeding.

Though I'm trained to their pH's and oxygen
   levels this
      is a lay practice of my own
care and feeding   They live in
   a timeless solution of their histories
      the living broth of their other
lives, their dead, their brothers   I find
   something familial
      familiar in these small squares
these boxes buried in the public air
   of the aquarium,
      the slave atlantic's water,

blocked each into a plot
   water is one

[137]

with its everywhere:
the how many lost of the all of us
            brought here —
            in my wandering
going in door to door into
        the gathered ecologies keeping
            a watch out for the shark,
in what I bring   in this extra grace
        said   from some black thing
            to this fare
— get their care and feeding

        as if some hour
            in all employment living to give it
goes to their loss
        where without that sorry
            new york minute's
pause at ourselves in this country   we lose
        our colors   the gray side of money
            that pale
of ghosts flying   folds on our chests,
        and we float up
            fattened by work
that is emptied of the gain
        back of our lives.

They come from in between things
        through   as though
            between things shines a door   we sing
of the orisha
        I hear a singing on the other side
            of a door
singing going on behind the tanks
        heard on the public floor
            people invisibly at work
on public display
        their aquarium   parading the corps
            we've decorated as gods   thousands

[138]

of years unseen

that morning we woke when we had lost
    the attempt all our supplies everything
        but our lives   washed down
the river   left in a puddle
    a fish we only had to dish up
        out of its own
carapace   a shelled catfish
    Plecostomus   and here it was
        I see now   recognize
one of my samples I care for
    in this exhibit
        all that kept me

alive 'til we reached a village.

    Come back in from my own
        expeditions out   I know
the diving aboard landing of
    the plane
        made into the glittering night waters
that are
    the city   home

searching the long waving light refraction
    for its drawing of
        that African's face.

But the boys   they'll grow up
    in what only is a difference
        in this country   as if
starting the exhibit at a different door
    changed the subject:
        their mother white like many's

somewhere in our people here,
    their African
        black like a many's in
our American   peoples)
    father came over
        long after

the middle passage on a plane
    to school
        A whole new subject here.
But we sit down

    to Miles to Louis Armstrong
        over dinner
and later a little Lou Donaldson
    gets us
        dancing   our stuff.

5. seat

The erased unshined polish
    of a board
        that is a mind
unmet
    nor chaired into a seat
        of any solving,
gray with no answers

the slate smoothness of the cities' street
    education

That moving standing still
    we learn
        that rest is hanging on   no seat
keeping the strap
    and loop's flow open
        from around your neck
your foot out of the trap

The loss of grace complaint
    forgets we find footing
        accomplishment in that

6. *Dance, for the Balance of New Mexico*

We had driven until the land rover was in danger
of never being upright again at this height.

The cloud came through the window on the driver
side and out the passenger and stopped,

its center on the seat between.

To go further would have been to carry
black clown from Second Mesa's Butterfly Dance,

his foggy, white stripes   floating ash
across the blackened rocks

naked from a fire   his hardened body

We could hear the land rover strain, his screaming
laughter just before he'd leap through a complete

standing somersault, and we would halt
and float the truck for that moment he was air

in a sweated cloud of fear until he touched
the balance to the ground and put us down.

7. Flamenco Goyasques

We all have
    women we were born of

We all were dragged out &
    lined up against the sky

Know that
    Somebody here stood beside you

You put up your hands & you die

. . . .

Just in . . .
Just in word.

Word

of navigational
challenges

DESIGNED BY
SAMUEL RETSOV

TEXT: 11 PT SABON
TITLES: 20 PT DUMOUNT

ACID-FREE PAPER

PRINTED BY
MCNAUGHTON & GUNN